DREAM BIG

FOR KIDS

BOB GOFF AND **LINDSEY GOFF VIDUCICH**

ILLUSTRATED BY SIAN JAMES

An Imprint of Thomas Nelson

Dream Big for Kids

© 2022 Bob Goff and Lindsey Goff Viducich

Tommy Nelson, PO Box 141000, Nashville, TN 37214

Published in Nashville, Tennessee, by Tommy Nelson. Tommy Nelson is an imprint of Thomas Nelson. Thomas Nelson is a registered trademark of HarperCollins Christian Publishing, Inc.

The authors are represented by Alive Literary Agency, www.aliveliterary.com.

Tommy Nelson titles may be purchased in bulk for educational, business, fund-raising, or sales promotional use. For information, please email SpecialMarkets@ThomasNelson.com.

ISBN 978-1-4002-2092-2 (eBook)
ISBN 978-1-4002-2089-2 (HC)

Library of Congress Cataloging-in-Publication Data is on file.

Written by Bob Goff and Lindsey Goff Viducich

Illustrated by Sian James

Printed in Malaysia
22 23 24 25 26 IMG 6 5 4 3 2 1

Mfr: IMG / Selangor, Malaysia / September 2022 / PO #9589890

To the next generation of big dreamers.

When you're snuggled in bed under a cozy blanket, fast asleep, your imagination takes over and creates wonderful stories. In your dreams, you might have superpowers that let you fly over the tallest buildings. Or you may discover new parts of the world on an extraordinary adventure.

Those are wild and wonderful dreams, but did you know some of the best dreams come when you're wide awake? These dreams are the fantastic hopes you have for yourself and those around you, and God places these dreams inside each of us!

THE WRIGHT BROTHERS

People throughout history have dreamed about amazing things they wanted to do with their lives.

An enslaved woman named Harriet Tubman dreamed of helping others escape slavery, and she eventually led many people to freedom.

Two brothers, Wilbur and Orville Wright, dreamed of flying high above the clouds, and they made the world's first successful powered airplane.

As a young girl, Malala Yousafzai dreamed of helping girls in her country have an education just like the boys her age, and she spoke up about this need, even when it put her in danger.

These people were once kids just like you, and they followed their big dreams. Because they did, they changed the world.

God has given you big, amazing dreams too. You see, the Bible says God made you in His image. Our creative God put a whole lot of who He is into who you are, which means He filled you up to the tip-top with creativity. Your creativity helps you dream big dreams—dreams that *matter*—daytime dreams that are even better than the ones you have when you're asleep. And here is the exciting part: you don't have to wait until you are a grown-up to start living these dreams! You can start right now!

Dreams come in different shapes and sizes, and they hardly ever look the same. It's kind of like how no one's fingerprints are the same and how no two snowflakes are alike. A dream isn't big because it's loud and flashy and gets a lot of attention. What makes something a big dream is the way it reflects the one-of-a-kind person God created you to be and the way it leaves an impact on the people God loves—which is everybody!

Maybe you dream of exploring the world. Perhaps you like to dig in your family garden, hike through the woods, or swim across the lake. People with this big dream use these adventures to draw attention to things that are sometimes overlooked. Maybe you will be a big dreamer who helps everyone understand how important it is to enjoy and take care of our beautiful planet!

Maybe you dream of building a community. If you love when your friends and family spend time together and this makes you smile inside and out, you can look for ways to make that happen. Do you know your neighbors? Do you ask the new kid to play with you? People with this great big dream help everyone around them feel welcome and loved. Keep an eye out for someone who could use a friend and invite them to spend time with you. You are a community builder!

Maybe you dream of inspiring others. Are you the kind of person who notices your friends' superpowers, even when they don't see those superpowers in themselves? You might see beautiful but overlooked things in the people around you. If you do, you have a gift! These dreamers sometimes become teachers or coaches and help others reach their own goals and dreams. Does this sound like you?

Maybe you dream of encouraging people. When someone is down, do you like to cheer them up? Do you like to say kind words to make people smile? Isn't it fun to make someone feel special? Each encouraging word you say is like a balloon you hand to a friend that lifts their spirits up! Write a song or book or poem to brighten someone's day. They will love it, and so will you!

Maybe you dream of helping people feel better. When you see a friend fall down, do you run to check on them and get them a bandage? Do you look for ways to take care of your friends when they feel sick? You may have big dreams about fighting sickness as a doctor or a nurse or a scientist who helps others stay healthy. These big dreamers make it so there is less pain in the world. You could be one of them!

Maybe you dream of making the world a fairer place. If you see someone being left out of a game on the playground, you might say, "Let's make sure everyone can join!" People like you speak up for those with smaller voices, share beautiful things with those who don't have as much, and invite those left on the sidelines to come and play. You stand up for what is right and good and stick up for those who are treated unfairly.

No matter what it looks like, each dream matters.
Right now, and as you continue to grow up, you can
practice using your gifts and explore your interests to
discover what beautiful dream God has in store for you.

God has given one big dream to everyone, and it's called love. In fact, Jesus said the biggest dream you could ever have is to love Him and the people He made. No matter what dream God gives you, you can use it to share His love with the whole world. So maybe you'll invent something amazing to make life a little better for people in need, or maybe you'll find a new way to help people heal a little faster from sickness. Maybe you'll help people feel like they belong. Whatever you do, you have the chance to pass on God's love, and that is always the best kind of dream.

People throughout history have dreamed big dreams, from leading countries to being good friends to their neighbors.

Pay attention to the things that spark your imagination—things that make you feel extra alive—to help you figure out God's big dreams for you. Always keep your eyes open for what could be possible!

Sometimes dreaming is hard. Some dreams are tougher than others, and not all dreams work out how we expect. The biggest dreams often take the most patience and hardest work, and sometimes you need some help. That's why God put people in your life who love you and want to help you! Don't be afraid to chase your dreams, because each dream will teach you something more about yourself and about God.

As people grow up, they sometimes forget about following their dreams. They forget they have something really special to bring to the world and that God made them for a purpose. But following those dreams is the most exciting adventure you could ever be a part of.

Keep dreaming your great big dreams and encourage others to remember to chase theirs too!

Your wonderful, creative dreams matter. They might be the very things God wants to use to make the world a better place. So what is your dream? Make sure you tell everyone what it is and get started. The world needs what only you can bring— your big dreams!